NOAH'S ARK DAYCARE
P.O. BOX 277
CAYUGA, IN 47928

I'm Glad I'm Me!

written by Frances Carfi Matranga

illustrated by Joanne (Jodi) McCallum

To my grandson, Nicky,
with love

Library of Congress Catalog Card Number 90-72094
© 1991. The STANDARD PUBLISHING Company, Cincinnati, Ohio
Division of STANDEX INTERNATIONAL Corporation. Printed in U.S.A.

I'm glad I'm not a busy ant
Just working all the day.
To work is good, but what about
A little time to play.

I'm glad I'm not a kitten
    Who "meows" for everything.
I like to talk and whisper;
    I like to hum and sing.

I'm glad I'm not a turtle
  With my house stuck onto me.
I couldn't hop and skip and run
  Or climb up in a tree.

I'm glad I'm not a pack rat
    That hoards all kinds of junk,
And am I glad that I am not
    A stinky little skunk!

I'm glad I'm not a penguin
In a land of snow and ice;
With no trees or grass, no flowers
That smell so very nice.

I'm glad I'm not an owl
That only flies at night
And has to sleep in daytime—
Oh, no! I like the light.

I'm glad I'm not a dolphin
    Living in the sea.
I'd have to swim and swim and SWIM.
    How tiring that would be.

I'm glad I'm not a tiger.
   Raw meat is all I'd eat.
No fruit or cake or ice cream.
   I'd get no special treat.

I'm glad I'm not a camel
   With a funny-looking hump
And a face that isn't friendly.
   Is a camel just a grump?

I'm glad I'm not a tall giraffe
    Without a scarf and coat.
If I caught cold inside my neck
    I'd have a HUGE sore throat!

I'm glad I'm not a crocodile
With scary, toothy grin.
I wouldn't like to be all green
With bumpy, scaly skin.

I'm really glad that I'm a kid.
It's what I want to be.
I'm glad to have my mom and dad
And GLAD God made me, ME!